Pame

NEW & SEL:

Guy—

Merci beaucoup

Pamela Brown

Reims 1992

110 Denison St
Camperdown   NSW 2050
557 1266

Pamela Brown lives in Sydney. Her work as a poet has been interrelated with her work as a performer, artist, filmmaker, teacher, printer and publisher. A selection of her writing is currently being translated into French.

Pamela Brown's **Selected Poems 1971 - 1982** collected the best from seven earlier, now out of print books: **Sureblock, Cocabola's Funny Picture Book, Automatic Sad, Correspondences, Cafe Sport, Country & Eastern** and **Small Blue View**.

Selected Poems 1971 - 1982 is now also out of print. This **New & Selected Poems** updates that edition with the inclusion of work from her prose collection **Keep It Quiet** and five new poems.

NEW &
SELECTED
POEMS

Pamela Brown

WILD & WOOLLEY
SYDNEY

Published by Wild & Woolley Pty. Ltd.
P.O. Box 41, Glebe NSW 2037.

Cover Painting: Jan Mackay
Cover Design: Kent Whitmore
Text Format: Pat Woolley
Printed by: Globe Press, Melbourne
                     Made in Australia

The prose in the section KEEP IT QUIET is a selection from the book of the same name, Sea Cruise Books, Sydney, 1987. Poems from the earlier SELECTED POEMS were edited by Barbara Brooks. The book was produced by Redress Press, published by Wild & Woolley, Sydney, 1983. LOCAL POEM and IN THE DARK were first published in *Cargo* magazine. THE LONG YEARS, ROMAN RED and THIS PLACE first appeared in *Otis Rush* magazine.

CIP
Brown, Pamela, 1948-
  New & selected poems.

  ISBN 0 909331 91 X.

A821.3

Arts by Australians
Australia Council

Publication assisted by the Australia Council, the Australian Government's arts funding and advisory body.

CONTENTS

CAFE SPORT Poems 1975 - 1978

CORRESPONDENCES

COUNTRY AND EASTERN

INTRODUCTION

I have a stray piece of notepaper in the archives, a note in my handwriting which says, 'Kindness begins out of desperation.'

'Not always,' has been written in pencil underneath. It is an annotation by Pamela Brown. I don't remember either of us writing this. It would have been on one of the many afternoon-days and evening-nights that we've spent together discussing ART, LIFE, CULTURE and WINE, not necessarily in that order.

I mention this by way of saying that I know Pamela Brown well, and in many moods. But none of this accumulated and shared experience is ever quite enough to prepare me for reading a recently written poem or a fresh collection of Pamela's work. Her writing simply takes my breath away, like being winded. And then it takes me a certain period of time to catch up.

For a start, and this is something that is often not noticed, her work displays a remarkable elegance. I think she'd rather die than publish something shoddy. In case this sounds too serious, Pamela has the same attitude to shoes. She also has one of the most acute ears for language of anyone who is presently writing here, but again, this faculty is not subservient to only lofty aims. I remember her delight once at a poem of hers being quoted: it was not so much the quote that mattered but the fact that the Sydney Morning Herald had printed the word 'boing' for the first time.

Wit, precision, word-play, technical proficiency, experimentation - these are all aspects that I enjoy about Pamela's work and they are there in abundance. But they are not the full accomplishment of her immense talent as a poet. Art must stimulate more than the senses.

In 1986, after Pamela had returned from Europe, she told me of her trip to Pompeii. Both Naples and Pompeii hold an emotional charge for me so I was eager for a report. Pamela told me about the house of the poet, the cast of a lava-trapped chained dog - she found the whole place unbearably sad. When I went there a couple of years later I felt this sadness more acutely than I would have otherwise. Our attitude towards history is very different, so much so that I suspect that Pamela doesn't really like the idea of history at all. And I don't have the humanity that she has for the dead. Being in Pompeii reminded me of 'A Thousand Tears,' one of the most moving poems in our language, and that confluence is one of the reasons why art is so important to me.

Pamela does not confuse art with life. Her writing does not feed, like some hungry vulture, off the flesh of her experiences. Which is not to say that she doesn't let it all hang out because she does do that, at parties, in arguments, in street demonstrations, sometimes even in her writing.

Don't forget that she has lived through and survived the upheavals of the 1960s and 1970s - drugs, feminism, rock'n'roll, hope, idealism, love. The earlier poems in this book are the echoes carried from this period. And she is not one of those writers whose art is forever in danger of sending her mad. She is too much of a realist for that.

Pamela is equally not a dispassionate observer. She'd hate it if anyone read her poems and concluded that somehow they were a record of the times. She's not a watcher from a cast iron anything, and sometimes she's not even a good listener, for she is too impulsive not to be involved. You can't sit still in a corner and just look when the world around you demands an answer, or a commitment.

Commitment has become a very strange word. It has been grossly devalued, broken, sent to the graveyard, like many words these days. Some of them have managed to cling on, barely alive, on the outskirts. Like Truth, sent to end its days breaking stones in the Gulag with Idealism, coughing its lungs out. And Morality, planning revenge and egging Poetry on, quoting the words of a peasant woman to the Russian poet Akhmatova, 'You are a Poet. You must remember this and one day write it down.'

We are no different in Australia in our devaluation. None of the most valuable things in our culture are cost effective. None of them can be traded, sold, accumulate money in the bank or lower the balance of payments. They can't even pay the dentist or bring down a government. If something becomes worthless it doesn't matter where it's coming from or where it's been.

I don't think that Pamela in her writing wants to hold up a mirror to reality. I don't think she even wants to interpret the world. Nor does she really think that her poems can lead to much change, though she wouldn't be an anarchist if she didn't secretly entertain that hope. Rather, her poems are like annotations brought back from the edges of experience. I like to think of them as bits of graffiti on the crumbling walls of whatever culture it is we live in.

You cannot be a poet without politics. It shocks me that people are often surprised by that statement. Can poets lie? If they do, they cease to be poets. Simple. I won't even try to define what Pamela's politics are - the poems themselves can do that. But what I do want to draw attention to is something that is not immediately obvious to readers of this book.

Pamela is a staunch supporter of small presses in Australia, so much so that all of her nine books have been published this way. Partly it is a way of maintaining control over her own product, and partly it is a hangover from the do-it-yourself philosophy of the 1960s. And it is also an important political statement.

Writing from New York in May 1984, fellow-poet Kate Jennings said in her introduction to the first edition of 'Selected Poems' that Pamela Brown's story 'isn't over yet: this is only her first "Selected Poems."' Well, welcome to Pamela's second 'Selected Poems.' I'm very pleased to have been asked to write this introduction. But it probably won't stop me from standing on street corners saying to startled passers-by, 'Read this book, it'll move you.'

Sasha Soldatow
Sydney 1990

SUREBLOCK
POEMS 1971 - 1972

who is this guy
who walks into the house
with an immediate opinion
of herman hesse and advice
on how to cook the rice?

An academic death
we never stopped to mourn
something else / apollinaire /
was there to take us limping
down the broadway of the brain
now we listen to nonthought
android news reports and documentaries
from the radio with no last truth

monsieur artaud visits our breakfasts
of red and blue molecules
scribbled on scrapbook pages.

THE RED COCACOLA BOTTLE

that we perform in syndicates
became obvious
when, while on weeks away
we found ourselves creating
some very unified notions

i spent the winter stoned
and decided on a pair
of gymboots

boiling up vermilion
in our workshops
to make a measure
on the world supply
of cocacola
and other works of heart;
desire in our dreams
and wistfulness.
all the time
i was wearing
the kind of shoes
that being alive
makes so dirty.

J JOPLIN J HENDRIX L BRUCE
B JONES R FARINA
N CASSADY

the words of our names have been dropped and
broken.
we did it ourselves / our tongues were swollen,
too heavy with speech

our tables and chairs are on the way home
disguised as furniture, somebody else's

our bodies have turned.

i have taken the house and painted it yellow,
my disneyland eyes are guarding the walls

i have invented a world called motorbike blue
where nobody needs,
where nobody dies,
ever, really.

POEM ALIVE / STRANGE

'and now denver is lonely for her hero'
Allen Ginsberg

we have seen the puppet show
and do not hurry any more . . .

washing the dirt from the snow . . .
shaping the sable hair lashlight . . .
making the dot after dot before dot line . . .

AUTOMATIC / RAT LANDS / sleeping / RAILWAY
cry for the secret hero / HOWL

put out the stars
body drowned / benzedrine / tequila

CASSADY IS DEAD

he does not hurry any more

KOMIK POLITIK / UNDERSTAND

demonstrations
should be expressions of
frustrations / SHIT

are comic politics like
richard nixon as daffy duck
with a name like dingle dick?
are they provotariat chickens
in flash gorton's face /
televised nationally / serialised
for radio.

something like being on the same
       WAVELENGTH
       for some time

rapunzel in government house
letting down her hair
letting off / STEAM

the phantom poet / FALLING
crashing to the floor
in broken words / she almost
blows her avant garde
and brings the meetings down

hanoi hannah rolls over in
the graveyard / SCREAM / a barricade

STRAIGHT ALL THE LENGTH
OF ME LONG

balcony boys
mothering their motors
and eating saveloys

ankle sox
& polka dots

700 teatowels marching backwards
up lygon street.

SUREBLOCK

it was midnight friday
when cattle annie came
to my house . . .
we had just eaten tacos
and cups of rosehip tea
for our sureblocked heads . . .
she came in the kitchen
with her shotgun
and her riding boots
and blew a hole
right through
the early kooka oven door.

LITTLE BREECHES

little breeches
unbuckled her gunbelt
and let it drop down
on a stack of national geographics;
putting a finger to her nose
she said "gimme a sandwich
with cream cheese and jam"
i did that,
a big thick sandwich.
she took out a roll of tape
and stuck the sandwich
over the hole
in the early kooka oven door.

we blew a joint
which got me very frightened
of this weird woman
who lopes along bootfooted
shootin' it up.
makin' a ruckus.

BLOWN FUSES

painting my riding boots glossmasta tangerine
with the electric radiator
and hank williams making it sad
to be here in the kitchen
rolling my own tobacco cigarettes.
stoned. a long way south of home.

blown fuses make the living cold
like going up and asking you
to wire my heart
to your electric dream.

it gets ridiculous to owe yourself a memory
makes you think you can't do
without some sort of symbols.

A POEM FOR CAPTAIN PATCHES AND I
DON'T SUPPOSE HE'LL READ IT

so i guess it's not my bag
to bead a pattern from your trials,
you see, you've heard my sleeping talk.
in early light i watched you laughing
when you told me things i'd done.

we are criminals in search of flowers.
natural. checking chinese gardens
for smoke and sacred vegetables.
so close to time there is no space for dreaming.

and i plead for some abstraction
to steal my thoughts away from me
but all you show is fast and real.
and somewhere lost. without imagination.
and the crystal you believe in,
'watch me now' it seems to cry
'i am pretty. tiresome. lonely.'

with most things mirrored in your eyes
sometimes you find it hard to speak
but there are no sounds in the sunflecked tide
and you have a friend in that.
it would be safe to simply swim away.

outside it's turned a little colder
and you wonder if you understand
anything at all about you.

and you once lost thirty dollars
and you never got it back.

COCABOLA'S FUNNY
PICTURE BOOK
POEMS 1973

SUMMER ICEBOX

those nights / summer / we sat
collating pornographic magazines
me stoned on snow
and wanting andy warhol,
you boozing and smiling
rolling your wonderful eyes;
pop culture children / summer
getting older all the time /
you telling me / your airbrushed eyes /
elvis presley regularly
injects silicone
into his tiny cheeks

in 'leave it to beaver'
the tv mom
pulls her cakes,
already frosted,
from her tv oven / in surry hills
disposable underwear
becomes a comment
on the transiency of shit stains;
and we are living in letratone,
lop-sided and lonesome

/ but most of all
i liked you
when you fell over
into bourbon and cement.
the dope turned to concrete
in my stomach /

we saw dennis hopper posing
for jim beam bourbon advertisements
in esquire magazine; probably
dangerous, health questionable.
myths questionable;
is leon russell a chauvinist?
does cilla black have a colostomy?

/ i fell in love. with you.
after you told me
you were once
a fourteen stone
teenage buttercup
stuck in the wildmouse
roller coaster carriage.
you had to go round twice
till they came
with crowbars and ropes.
you reduced to ten stone./

those nights / summer / i sat
reduced. tightly locked
in a pharmaceutical icebox.

A DREAM FOR CAPTAIN PATCHES

Hank Williams
had a party.
The refrigerator
was loaded
with Californian Poppy
hair oil
and
iced aftershave lotion.

HEY SHIT,
SHE SAID TO
NOBODY,
GRAVE DIGGERS
ARE CONCEPTUAL
ARTISTS.

THE LEAPS

MYOPIC POSSUMS
MYOPIC POSSUMS
MYOPIC POSSUMS

coked off my stoop

1966

the minties
thrown
at amateur hamlets
by
futurist schoolboys

LOVE / HERE IT IS

you wrapped my love in a sanforised rag
and put it out to sea . . .

to knowknowknow you is to know it never ends
from flushing the hidden meanings down
your cheeks from your flashing eyes
to carrying you out like a caryatid
in catastrophes we make ourselves

you wrapped me tight in a trombone knot
and put me all at sea . . .

AUTOMATIC SAD
POEMS 1974

ACADEMIC

he may be brilliant
at writing
the southern end
of sentences.
he cannot calculate
the yarrow straws
or understand
the readout.

CRAZY ENOUGH

crazy enough
to read the poem
and hear it
sound crazy

crazy enough
to tear to shreds
ten dollar bills
with
nothing in the pockets
nothing in the can

crazy enough
to fall to sleep
in the middle
of the suicides

crazy enough.

SHINS

i am close to
you?
i am closed too.
i am closer to
the moon
than
you.
your shins
are not
fantastic.

35mm black and white

a spoon full
of dead blowflies
on a window sill.

TURN DOWN MY F-STOPS

turn down my f-stops.
deep image blue
you blind me with bogart
two hours tough.

POEM FOR THE CHILDREN OF 1948

together, my friends.
together
we have reached
the age
of dental decay.

NIAGARA CAFE. GUNDAGAI

eating too many songs.
sad cows.
pension food.

PANACEA

endomorph.
ectomorph.
mesomorph.

shotamorph?

BLUES IN A

i saw you lose
your cigarette.
drunk. you were
nodding out
on a blues in A.

TRUE CONFESSION

once
i became
a cupboard reader.
was it a western
or pol magazine?

DOUBLE ADAPTORS

you thought i looked accessible
with my hair blowing on the wind.

i stood next to an electric fan.

you said you loved narcotics.

1931 - 32
cobalt blue

1974.
the scream
between
the blade
and
the throat.

HONKY TONK SUNSET

the chickens.

the guitar.

the chickenshit.

the lid
of the can
suspended
for the rifle.

the fence.

the chickens.

the guitar.

the chickenshit.

THE MEANEST MAN ON THE RANGE

the meanest man on the range
asks me to stay with him.

over his shoulder
a steam engine
floats across
emerald lake.

i'm not vacant.

no. i say.
you're too mean.
feeling sad.

always sad
about 'no.'

LISTEN COCKROACH

listen cockroach
if i wanted
a mexican sunrise
maybe i'd need you

down here / coming down
in the white walls,
the wrong brand
of paperbacks
and the humming fridge
singing   it
keeps on
talking to me
cockroach

movement cockroach
movement   one
move   cockroach

listen cockroach
mexican energy
frigidaire cockroach
watch it.

TREE FARM / MONBULK

the writing table
   supports
      two summer spiders.

moved out now
  to department of agriculture
   poster country.

the grass.   four feet high.
   beautiful.
wonderland of ticks and snakes.
evenings.   old songs.

kookaburras
  watch ploughed ridges
   change colour at sundown.

and no one working
  on the tree farm.

AUTOMATIC SAD

feeling like mountains / going off alone /
no very special person

random shoes.
imagine them filled / lying there
contorted
thinking something about
talking with you.
the pull of excuses.
thinking something about
bus stop telephones / meaningless greetings
under electricity wires splayed silver
over galvanised roofs,
thinking something about

feeling like mountains / going there alone/
no very special feeling.

CAFE SPORT
POEMS 1975 - 1978

SHE THOUGHT

there must be more to it
than climbing baobab trees
and drumming up eclipses
behind ayers rock / she thought.

halfwanting to run off
to the desert / where
she could eat herself.

but not my friends / she thought

kissing the panelvan goodbye.

AEROGRAMME BLUE

somehow
    there are symbols.
letters. paintings. haircuts.
dream words.

your many sided face.
    your white white photographs.

tamarama / the matchbox series beach.
sad   you discover
some significance every seventh wave.
and peeling off another thread of skin
  i uncover my own deceptions.

three full moons.
    your many sided face.
       your ivory hands.

where do you go
when i turn from the tarmac
sighing and swallowing
the monstrous sky.

blue.   blue.
aerogramme blue.
wet sheets slap my dreams.
i am metal.   blue.

once i begin to make a poem
  the distances dissolve
          somehow.

EARLY THIS AFTERNOON

early this afternoon
 i saw you sitting
purple bruises on your white white neck

they are building again.
 i said.
red glass.   french glass.

you. the serpent queen.
gone to something easier.
some repetition. some passion.
i saw you seductive,
snatching orchids
from crocodile jaws.

they are building again.
the city is golden.
you have called me dead.

 i ask.   often.
 i ask about you.
 they say mostly
you are staying stoned.
 they say sometimes,
 when they sing to you,
you drape yourself with doubt.

 the city is silver
 a cool moon
 silhouettes your lover
taking the motorbike south.
 she has left you a song.

they are building again
 the city is rising
greywhite as an iceberg.

TROPICAL BLACK

all the nights are tropical black.
any night alone. tropical black.
india ink exploding
          black on black.

within this indolent latitude
you lunch together
on the febrile wastelands
of your lives.

i turn to ice skating
out on the rim / the shimmering perimeter.
keeping my wide angle on paradise
i take refuge in chemical sunsets.

you all shouting in the wings.
the maniac moon mocks you
as your fingernails screech on the window.

tropical black.   dirty rain.
lame dogs cower in the bathrooms.
venus smiles   her teeth gleam
like brand new blades.
any night alone is tropical black.

THE PHOTOGRAPH

the clock taps accompaniment
to the small sound of my breathing,
the sound of pen stroke on paper.

lifeless. still. midnight.

next to the clock
        the photograph.

your slender hand
   impressing your face.
greyblack tones.
you are doubtful. pensive.
in the photograph
you seem to wonder who to trust.

you were shaky then / i was stronger.
        tough poet image

now
dressed in washed out baby blue
i prop myself up with my shadow
and lean into an elusive centre.

lately,
        between you and me,
sometimes a turbulent ocean,
sometimes a soft veil of sadness

in this poem   i am asking
        for your trust.
the photograph my medium.

LOVE POEM

Abandoned
with the anachronism of old arguments,
i tug and tear the catgut strings
beyond my cricoid cartilage,
and
you go gently to the keys
and make blue music.

ALTERNATIVES

will we settle for swaying trees ocean sunsets
  stifled moons eclipsed dark mysteries
or skyscrapers / selling old coke bottles
        for cigarettes /
                        in the end?
will we sob under plastered terrace walls
          all night long
lamenting the desert the seas the hills.

close eyes and the shape of sheets.
  blue.   early winter skies.
dolphins glazing your sea eyes.
  downstairs
    the slow zombies
      mopdancing to dustnoises.

the occasional pinprick.
      heroin or acupuncture.

LAST DITCH / AFTER THE REVOLUTION

after the revolution
i wanted to play
the child rolling the elephant piano
down the long wide reverie.

after the revolution
i watched the women growing old
snatching at validity
in their need to re-experience
analyse the revolution

i crawled away,
tiny bitumen holes in my knees.
i lost the front of my head
under an oldsmobile dashboard.

RADIOPOEM. 1968

just call me angel of the morning angel.
just brush my teeth before you leave me baby.

VANISHING POINT

hypnotic flickerings

i meet your ghost   at sunset
    shouldering the window
       of a south bound train
your eyes reflect
      a watercolour sky

my own phantom
   is slipping poems under doors
      at three am

some things hold fast,
  it is life which repeats
        repeats
         repeats

i remember
    always searching
       for lost civilisations

old moths from old nights
    softly batting
     dust in my eyes,

i am small   i am small
    i have reached
     vanishing point.

KICKING WOMAN

kicking woman
  reading too many books
      at once
        out loud.
kicking woman
  once she talked
    for a thousand years.
took her tent to the desert,
       sat there staring
  described herself separately
as
kicking woman
  doesn't trust other women's feet,
    only their faces she says.
  she can remember
   almost everything,
and has had little to do
       with egypt
       or death.
kicking woman
  with oceans of notions
    goes on down
      to the white page,
kicks the shouting shit out of my words.

LEAVING

so now i have to pack my forests
    and baggages.
so now i have to pack my eagles
    and teardust.
and the way you talked to overflow.
and the way you were so fast to change
    into your many shades of sorrow.
and the way you swept the miracles
    away from your shabby gentility.
and the way you trembled
    as you chose the latest props.

so hello attache case face.
hello briefcase face.
hello screaming suitcase.

DYNAMITE BLUES

monosyllabic trickster
when you cry   you only cry
   nothing more
by the telephone you cry
   and nothing more
oh
so you drinkin' dynamite
         tonight.

RAIN

rain on your hysteria.
you lie low in the undertow
of the bedrooms of the frightened.

i send you signals.
fooling wet-wicked flares.
    some display.
some hurricane your hysteria.

i paint my nails blood red.
blow cool on my nails.

so rain away rain.

YOU ARE A BRANDNEW
PHOTOGRAPHIC PRINT TO ME

lying on the floor like that
  all wet with tears and chemicals
    drying out under my hot breath

i am trapped by my image of your image.

  i would like to
  i would really like to

my fingers have been yellowed
              by your developments.

i am going to slip you
      into this black packet

  you won't grow old there
  you'd never grow old there.

THE MACROBIONIC WOMAN

the macrobionic woman
 eating terylene rice
  spits her kernels
   on white pile carpets

playing punk dyke all weekend
 trying to toughen the pericardium.
       she is so fragile.
sometimes scoots along the dunes
  slips down the ski slopes
   never cracking her bones / her heart
          already cracked.
she is young and she is accumulating memories
       fast as snowballs
          released by sisyphus / lost his grip.

the macrobionic woman
   laughs too loud   always   laughs too loud.

YOU SOMETIMES

you sing about dancers.
you write like hemingway.
you sometimes forgive me, buy champagne.

i heel your boots / glaze your windows
  colour your ceiling / drive your car
       carry your boxes.

you polish my coins.

AND OF COURSE

and of course
if i would leave myself alone long enough
if i would cease this careful vigil
watching the foxes run through your hair
the red fox   the silver fox

and of course i will put your boy in a poem
i will have him skid and slide
        and skin his knees.
i will flatten your tyres before morning
        so you have no escape.
i will steal all the cans of coloured paint
        you might hope to use
        to perfect your changes

and of course
as you use my imagination
i still cannot find the word for you

and of course
you'll always stand on the other side
of the long parade / the carnival
the courtroom circus / precise protected prosecutors
the other side of a thousand restaurants
    a thousand marxist classes
    a thousand gin glasses
the other side of every country and western song
    ever recorded
the other side of every mythical rainbow
your boyfriend might describe
on your bedroom wall

and of course   there are the times
    i wait by the stereo
feeling like a dumped car
lying in the wrecking yard
my mouth like crumpled alloy
while you stand   ready to kiss my eyes
on the other side of every monstrous bookcase
    every ancient building
every dream where i might walk away from you
while you fuck with the fascist boyos

and of course i have given up driving cars

and of course   i have collapsed
i have given myself hepatitis tuberculosis

and of course   i have finally become
    the wholly romantic poet.

SLEEP POEM

i was asleep at the time

you crawled through my room
on your way to the dance floor.

you do not like my shoe
and you tell me you do not.

i am asleep at the time.

you say grim joke.
i say cheap trick.

that's life. i go to sleep.

G'DAY RIFLEHEAD

g'day riflehead.

i see you shot the mirrors down
while i slept like a splinter.

you were a sheet to me.
i ripped you up for rags.
made myself a bandage.

PHONE ME IN CARE OF THE BLUES

phone me in care of the blues.

all this talk of how it could be.
sometimes my cunt is throbbing
like a bass guitar.

you get the people worried for you.
you slip their hearts a song.

then you take them in.
it is your skin which takes them in.
they cling to you like wet cotton clings.

you phone me from six hundred miles.
oh you mean to say you're lonely now.

sure.   i'll wait at the tarmac.
sure.   i'll lunch with you.
here   i've made this handgrenade sandwich

MEMOIRS OF A DUTIFUL DOG

sometimes   i feel
like a country and western dog.

here girl   lick my fingers
here girl   nuzzle my nipples
here girl   fetch my songbook
               fetch my plectrum

if i could drive
   my dog teeth through
       to you.

here girl   speak up
               speak up.

WESTMORELAND STREET POEM

all morning   i lie in bed
reading kate jennings poems
searching for clues
to alcohol / life in the ghetto
to loving the blues of loving.

they say she always cooked too fast.
burned the chips.   impatient.
always stoking the gasflames in her veins.

i wonder if kate jennings watched
these patterned skin leopard slugs
sliding slowly along the sills,
whether she performed chemical murders
scalding their backs with burning salt.

all afternoon   i lie in bed
reading. writing this poem. drinking pernod.
the slugs have left trails on the carpet.
the roaches have eaten the gold dust.
the poems are wandering home.

LAMINEX RADIO

she is telling me what to do.
don't visit the ochre tablelands,
there are books to read.
read only peaceful books.

i lean on the laminex radio.
no more tabletops to mop.
thinking   if i could take
her footprints from the snow.

i ask her to come to the forest,
tearing up heartshaped shadows
        in the half light
while she continues talking
telling me   she cannot breathe
unless the air is stuffed
            to stopping point
                with words.

she is telling me to sleep.
i do not want to lose sight
            of her sounds.

GREAT TROUBLES

and now you cannot be with me.

i vomit in gardens.
i poison myself in brandy.

you have gone to the sea
to colour your photographs.

great troubles.
predators leap to tell me
you are not in my life.

i am terrified of friends.
i am terrified of strangers.
a smooth skinned girl pursues me.

i am desperate to drive to the sea.

today i saw a dog
with two limbs broken.

TONIGHT YOU ARE

tonight i could walk any stret
i could terrify the tough glebe boys
stashing stolen radios in blind backlanes.

     tonight i am tall
tonight you are   tonight you are

i could
hurl anything i have   anything i have
    over the cliffs.
shake off the world shoot through a masterpiece.
    laugh up a highrise building

tonight
   i could talk too fast forever
   never hear the other sides
not even listen   not even care

you asked
   how far we would dare to take this thing.
   tonight   i stretch all limits

tonight you are   tonight you are.

bullet holes in the windows.
secondhand hotel furniture.

crying there and singing some.

i only wanted
to be your harmonica.
y'see. i only wanted
to play for you.

heard you had the blues.
couldn't stand a push.

QUEEN OF THE SQUATS

about growth; one part of this woman is shrinking.

i walk the streets lost in her monologue. follow her
down to the radio station. she is saying 'and if they
give me the airwaves i'll be sure to say everything.'

she tells the man on the door he looks like wolfman
jack and he says 'sure kid, and you go and tell misty
to play dead.' nobody laughs. the man on the door
takes her guitar and i want to smash plate glass
windows, hotwire white jaguars and speed away
from the queen of the squats forever.

in the studio corridor she tells me love is chemistry,
love is something alchemical. i question myself 'what
do i think i think?' and then 'so what' i say 'i've been
in and out of romantic swimming pools. you just end
up with chlorine in your eyes' and i turn and run
crazy out of the building.

i catch a taxi home. i am intact now. i turn on the
radio. i take out a lead pencil. i write 'cobalt blue' on
the wall in very small round letters. intact. not
known at this address. as i fall asleep i can hear the
queen of the squats raving, half drunk, at that old
cardboard dime, the moon.

STEREO TYPES

this was a listless linda ronstadt romance.
no chipped fingernails. everything polite.
everything perfect.   love is a rose
and all the right wines.

she switched off the bedside light.
he stepped quickly out of his underpants.
he bent to light the candle
then he climbed up on her
and they fucked
and they came together
and they moaned in harmony in the key of C
afterwards he put a record on the stereo.
she took out two blue kleenex tissues.
she wiped her cunt and handed him the other tissue.
he wiped his cock.
listless linda sang: 'although he may be cute
                    he's just a substitute
                    and you're the permanent one.'
he took out a sleeping pill and snapped it in two.
he swallowed half and handed her the other half.
she swallowed it
and they slept
and they had forgotten
all previous unstained involvements

in the morning they showered, dressed, ate breakfast.
she picked up her briefcase. he picked up his.
he kissed her on the forehead,
she said, 'i'll phone you.'
he drove to the office. she walked to the university.
love is a rose is a rose is a rose.

THIS OLD ANGEL

'the angels are older.
they know not to wait up for the sun.'

- Jackson Browne

snakes   silverbellied
    blackbacked snakes
slip smooth   close to my ankles
        as i track
the shadowed grasses
            of my unconscious

out here   this primal wilderness.
    voices are nothing but phantoms
        whispering elegant lies.

my trouble   out here   is memory.
    i remember myself
    as a powerful creature,
    an archangel of darkness
        dancing with anubis,
taking to mystery
    with the passion of a desperado.

there was learning in the dance
    and now
        this old angel
        rustles softly through the grasses
            out on the boundary.

the longer i write poems for you
the shorter they become.

THREE SUMMERS

Stanthorpe 1953
every night lulled to sleep by the hum of the
generator. every day riding on the beat-up tractor
through the orchard. kevin picks plums from the
trees and gives them to me. one of his legs is bent.
kevin doesn't walk straight. he has a pet sheep.
someone tells me kevin is my second cousin. i don't
like kevin. i like his sheep.

Darling Downs 1955
red dirt dust storms. old rutledge the drunk asleep
under the weatherboard church down near the creek.
flies on farmers' faces. hot dry winds over pale
yellow wheatfields blanched out by the sun. magpies
swooping and diving at my brother in the paddock.
old rutledge opens one eye; just the kids looking for
yabbies.

Chinchilla 1958
a plaited leather stockwhip and several branding
irons hang on the back verandah. the trucks rumble
the cattle to the sales. the auctioneer speaks in
tongues. once in a while we wade through waist high
paspalum and sunflowers. go down to the railway
line. wait for the goods train. the engine driver
shouts and waves and then moves on to somewhere
we've never been. this can always be counted on.

CORRESPONDENCES
PROSE-POEMS 1977 - 1978

ALL ROADS LEAD TO ALBUM COVER LANDSCAPES

i once felt a little foolish with my eyes wide open
obviously searching the western deserts.
searching for you.

so i followed the pull of the moon. drove to the
coast. looking for you.

they had constantly measured the size of your
psychic blemishes. they told me you had shattered
your own glass heart. there was a vacancy. it was as
if we had never touched. you had jumped from the
seventh floor window.

they held a photographic exhibition for your death.
jude and i played your old favourites. drank
overproof all the long night long. in the morning
i drove further along the coast.

all roads lead to album cover landscapes.

AT FIRST

at first, you came with tears and coloured stones.
we offered each other real life. three dimensional
loving. my tongue gently sucking your sweetness.
your hands turning my skin.

tonight the sun sets bloodblue across the sky,
matching my memory of the bruises. all those
sunsets. symbolic distractions from the blades
we used to wield in frenzied passion. i would
plead and loathe myself for pleading. there was
something incomplete.

you were desperately concerned with the makings
of yourself. you continued the search. the guitarist.
the actress. the travellers were there. closing in on
summer. gunbelts in the corner. you specialised
your knowledge. you concentrated on mirrors.
you had to tell them how they mirrored each other.

reluctantly, i began to pile the rubble. black rocks
in my mouth. you took yourself to icy skies. and
came back to tell me it was no longer PRACTICAL
to be with me. i PRACTICALLY exploded.

storm breaks.   memory shakes.
i have no need of practicality.
i dare to swim in my own hot blood.

LETTER TO A GHOST RIDER

once, trailing my lips around your neck, i thought
i would fashion a rhinestone studded noose.
i swallowed spansules containing clocks, coins and
automobile rhythms. absorbed in my motivation
to pin your effigy with cold steel needles.

i never believed you. i shot you up with the residue
and you took me riding. the corner came too fast
for you. the bike spun out. the scar on my hand
took the shape of a continent where i longed to
travel. away from you. myself. the common
fantasy you insisted we shared.

i heard you went south. passed right through my
city on your way. 'an ambulance can only go so fast.'

ONE FOR PATTI SMITH

one of my friends lost her mind in nineteenth
century novels. i tried to have her take a cure.
i offered your books. i said here are wild dog hotel
poems. cocaine and cooked dog. i said. wild street.
totally present words. here take them they're for
you. read them now please.

once, my lover promised to fly you from new york.
on my birthday. i knew you'd find me tedious.
impervious to perversity. another day another fan.
my lover was full of empty promises and no money
anyway.

ps. i never had the ramones, stones, fabian forte or
anyone else on my wall.

LETTER FOR THE ROCKABILLY RESEARCHER

you took my thin scratchings, called them 'poems',
and embraced them. i was only half wherever i was.

and when i heard you say the stars were dead
i was afraid. would you postcard me off.
place me somewhere at the end of the file
where i might assist the others in creating dust.

i have kept the blinds drawn for several days now.
the stars are dead you say.
i cannot stand to see the stars.
i have bruised all illusions. you have gone your way.

and i want so much to call you back.
to kiss you in library elevators.
walk easy with you in graceful parks.
see you ride wild horses across the sand.

overpowered by your songs,
sometimes i dream you shout at me.
you retreat to discovering the past.

we love to search the diaries of our friends
for mention of ourselves.

THE DEAR JOHN LETTER

between the sugar and the short black
something like grief   came over me

it was your cafe moralism.
from london to canada and back
to coaldust. lungs full of dead gymboots.
the cost of this and the cost of that.
the gold bands on white filtered cigarettes.

stranded there   enormous. sad.
grey   on the fringe of the neon.

in the bathroom
i noticed the dark rings under my eyes.
the deepening of the lines on my face.
the peoples palace towel on the rack.
          in the bathroom
i remembered the only morning of my life;
        i sat on a tiled verandah
        with a woman in a blue kimono.
        small white boxes of coloured slides
        scattered around us.   i was
        holding the slides to the sunlight.

lately   every change
had scared and changed me.
through the bathroom window
a fat girl walked slowly over to a fountain.

i would rather kick and shout
        than grieve like that.

COUNTRY AND EASTERN
POEMS & PROSE 1979 - 1980

CAPRICORNIA

the red moon rises over the lake
like a giant motel sign.
dead kangaroos.   hit and run
for miles and miles and sugarcane.
the neatest farms in the east.
and here i am in an o'nite van.

YEPPOON

down in the tea tree scrub the japanese corporation builds a resort for businessmen. they've bought the beach. the bush. the lagoon. the farms. the government. bought the spirit of the place.

in the torchlight we follow the pattern sandshoes make in the wet sand. way down the beach a jetty looking like a shipwreck in the dark. soft talk as we walk back. the sea slaps gently against our legs.

some distance north of brisbane. brisbane - i say 'city of no nostalgia' and remember a few things. high weatherboard houses where we lost so many summer days to sleep. late nights walking up the tram tracks in the empty centre of town and the police taking our names and address too many times.

here   the tent sides flap in the breeze. the long verandahs of all those shady hotels are behind us. the indigo blue night holds us now. on the beach.

INTERNATIONAL EXPERTS

when we get restless
we talk about
where we could go

we decide
london has had it
except for music.
madness.
marianne faithfull.
the selecter.
paris has had it
except for a few
memorable spots.
paul eluard.
gertrude stein.
sartre. semiology
and plastic bertrand
from belgium.

of course
we mention
new york.
the americans
are doing
all the writing
these days.

asia and india
are out of the question.
no package deal ashrams.
although japan
is interesting.
comics and posters.

really though
berlin
is the place to go.
fassbinder. brecht.
a politically
complex past.

experts.
micky met
sumo wrestlers
in japan
before america
and europe.
jill saw paris
and london
last year.

down in sydney
the air goes bad
and i fill up
with gases,
go to the movies,
buy books, a record
and a train ticket
to queensland.

WHAT DO YOU DO

what do you do. you are getting older
still feeling nostalgia and it's as intense
as ever. what do you do. you know
you'll check the impulse to phone
when you're drunk at two in the morning.
to hitch interstate or catch a train.
to just turn up. as you would
five or ten years ago. to just turn up
with dope and stories and you
haven't smoked dope for four years.

you are alone at the wheel with time
on your hands. driving at night
past old friends' houses. used to be
nights you were driving to be with them.
all that has changed. nobody visits.
the houses remain. what do you do.

you are watching tv with a drink
on the table. you are watching tv
but you do not belong there.

COLOURFUL ROZELLE

in the heatwave the young athlete struts about in his
green silk shorts. sweating and straining and up the
street an old man slings a hessian bag over his
shoulder. grubby and bent and probably loony. a boy
with transfers on his t-shirt slowly skateboards by the
girls leaning on the red brick wall. a hula hoop
clatters to the footpath. too hot to push today and the
doors are wide open at the welcome hotel.

and she is lugging that old camera to the bus stop to
catch the four forty one down to the sugar factory
where shimmers line the rooftop.

in the sultry night we hear the rumble of the shunting
in the railway yard. and i kiss the tender part of her
forehead. her cool temple and through the window
see the coral tree so still and dark and dropping into
sleep.

NOTHING CURED

In the afternoon we go to the cinema. She feels lonely. So she will fill the dangerous hours with images. A German film.

At sunset we steal leftover carafes from the tables on the Opera House terrace. We sit with our feet propped on the sea wall and we talk. She says she likes the bright blue block of flats across the harbour. We drink the stolen wine and watch the ferries crossing beneath the mammoth bridge. She says she thinks most lives are very ordinary - even the famous watch tv.

In the foyer we slump together on the vinyl couch. She looks up across the room and the sidney nolan mural seems to thunder down and thump her, turning her stomach. The vast wall repeats primitive crayon shapes. Graceless. Clumsy. Over and over the shapes of a shark in various colours in rows of squares. She thinks of processed food. This wall. Something about crates of tomato sauce stacked in a factory.

And so it goes and for a while it gets less lonely.

We walk down through the park to the narrow road running alongside the canal. The street light outlines palm trees against the dark blue sky. She says when she lived around here she used to call this place 'murder country' and as she says it her mind hears an ad asking her to come to marlboro country. There's a siding off the narrow road behind the railway bridge. There, in the siding, a young boy was raped and bashed to death with a rock.

The detectives door-knocked every house in the district questioning everyone. For months the suburb was littered with identikit posters of the wanted man. She remembers nights when she took that shortcut by the canal and how she would break into a run as she approached the railway bridge. Sometimes she had run all the way from Annandale to Glebe.

Tonight we say goodbye at the underpass.

She walks down the street past the slick car showroom. Two boys lean against the plate glass. They turn and make a kind of clicking call at her as she passes.

An old newspaper slaps at the footpath.
Lonely. It all returns. Nothing cured.

She turns the corner and sudden gaudy guitars blare out from the darkness in the empty street. A man shouts calypso crazy in time with the music. An old man in a big coat carrying a cassette tape recorder. He shouts the song, jubilant and urgent. Once before, she saw him in the supermarket with the precious tape recorder wrapped up in a plastic bag and someone's greatest hits playing loudly. He strides reckless down the road and doesn't look at her as they pass.

She pushes the gate. House in darkness. And inside the house it's lonely too. Dragging and dormant. If only she was terrified - somehow murder is such a simple fear.

MIDNIGHT SATURDAY

it's midnight saturday and i'm lying in the lounge
room watching some rock stars sing country romance
songs on the old black and white tv set with this
blackness creeping up the tube and flattening the
image so that the rock stars look very squat very fat.
it is an old videoclip and they are singing songs
which take me back three years. those songs were so
important then in summer when the evening skies
were soft and pearly through the doors which
overlooked the race track with the pale pink
grandstand and the grass neatly circumscribed by
white paling rails - a few trainers pacing the graceful
trotters in time with the music - and now in this
lounge room without the view they sound so bland all
these cowboy rock stars seem so limp so los angeles
and times have changed but for a moment i'm
missing that summer.

they sat on the back verandah. in the shade. like
narcolepts. fruit flies hovered around the muscat
bottle. they thought about taking the shotgun to the
river bank and ending everything.

they had all the time in the world and they couldn't
use it. slowly   they had become like that. they liked
to think about some time when their condition didn't
destroy their spirit and leave it at that.

they moved around in the city knocking on the doors
they once closed behind them. stood there like two
missing persons. listened like two posts.
then they turned away.

MOUNTAIN LAGOON

I
we are living our lives
as if we are on holiday.

long mornings
when we walk
to the lagoon
in the light rain.

the people around here
drive everywhere.
they say
there is either
too much rain
or too little
and,
in the orchards,
it's the same with money.

the things we do
are useful.
feeding chickens.
collecting wood.
patching the roof.

this afternoon,
every now and then,
i walk from the fireplace
to the window

peach trees across the road
sloping down to eucalypts
and beyond this - the vista
with white mist banked on the hills.

II
the room is blue.
today, in the room,
i consider this place.

for years i lived
in the middle
of everything i hated.
it felt great
to be part of the destruction
and to continue to live
as if i might prevent it.

the walk to work
past the soap factory,
coal piles, shunting yard,
container wharves,
the wheat silos across the water
and down harbour
the monstrous bridge.

i have come here
to the blue room,
the grey wattle outside,
to repair my losses,
to cover myself in air.

III
twice a week
there's the mail run.
huge wet hearts
fill the letterbox.

a handpainted postcard
of drunk people
out at night.

letters from friends,
family, flyers from
galleries, occasional
bills, bankcard statements

and once,
a home entertainment
questionnaire.

do you own
a television set,
stereo receiver,
videotape recorder,
slide projector?
do you
use them?
when?

big events
in the bush.

in the cool room we cut strawberry runners. we look terrific with dirt smudged faces and dirt on our clothes. peter brings in a live diamond python from the edge of the patch. and we handle this beautiful snake which is cool and dry to touch. after work i ride home on the bicycle past bright red maples and blade grass and rusty grevilleas - a colour we call 'werner herzog pink.'

DROUGHT

today i drank
  so much
     mineral water
     in the dry
        still heat

with the radio on
  the news and weather:
     "it's a drought"

the canvas
  on the chair
     fading fast
     and the leaves
        turning sere

so i drank
  mineral water
     tried two
        redhead
           match tricks

solved them both.

SO YOUNG

- for Micky Allan

if you were here
these are the things
i would tell you

and since you
are not here,
and since you
are, in fact,
at a party
in melbourne,
i'd like to
let you know
that i am thinking
small tonight,
my thoughts are
about the size
of the original
pk gum packet.

no big ideas

except   yesterday,
in the supermarket,
i noticed that
the canned
and powdered baby food
is shelved between
the canned
and dry cat food
and the canned
and dry dog food.
this told me
something
about life,

or life with
g j coles,
or life in richmond, nsw
which is, as you know,
fifteen hilly miles
from here,
and which is like
a small town
big suburb
with a few
historic leanings
towards the country,
with a local paper
which carries only
drink driving stories,
real estate deals
and rotary club gossip.

anyway   now
i will tell you
that tonight
i know
i am old enough
to have worn
a guy mitchell blue blouse,
and to have studied
parsing,
but
when you are here
'you make me feel'
(dionne warwick)
'so young'
(jo jo zep & the falcons).

A KIND OF TRAVELOGUE

- for Vivien Cielens

I
it is cold
  and mist everywhere
          here.

i move   in and out
    of a kind of
          malaise

shifting between
  certain memories
  and a certain notion
      of the future.

a few cars
  slide through the mud
    on the road
        outside

the drivers
  sometimes look across
          to this window.

II
there was talk
  of a place called
    'mount remarkable'
a suburb
  called
    'paradise'

a few connections
  like
     patsy cline.
we could remember
  two or three lines
        at least.

sarah said
  we were in
     'serious country.'
in the old grey rover
  motoring past
     the rocky river pistol club.
         (that seemed serious)

flat flat serious
  south australia.

the terrifying way
  you would turn
     away from the wheel
      to talk to us
      as if the rover
         drove itself.

anne and i
  took out our calculators
     and could not fathom
         kilometres to the litre
and anne
  is an expert
     in science fiction.

the pale blue horizon.

flocks of white birds.
  peppercorn trees.
    creekbeds flat with shale.

sometimes
  it was
    as if we came
      from somewhere
        in our pasts.

SMALL BLUE VIEW
POEMS 1981

A POEM ALMOST IN THE
COALCLIFF STYLE

- for Sal & Ken

the wind today
  is relentless from the south.
    turtleneck weather.
and, only yesterday - heatwave,
    sunburn, shorts.

but i am not going to describe
              the days here.
anyway
  i am leaving the district.

instead - days at your house.
    each back window
with its immense blue view,
  and the way you write it -
sal's clouds passing the past.
  and ken, in poems, playing records.
    then drinking coffee
      and drawing little clouds.
          (boing!)

and stories of visitors
  who run for the train,
    who wait
        until they hear it coming,
and some, until they **see** it
      up across the road
almost level with the kitchen door
        and **then** they run.

people i never imagine running,
  not thinking
    of any of your visitors
      as 'athletic'
(except leigh stokes -
  but then, he might not be fit,
              just energetic.)

micky and i
  drive to coalcliff
and always notice
  the ugly spots -
the 'hotel namatjira'
    at rooty hill,
the army camp
    at liverpool,
the reactor dome
    at lucas heights -
so that when we arrive
  we want to shout
'GREAT! THE GREAT BIG SEA!'
  which doesn't leave (not for
  a moment) until we do.

SHEER VENEER

the biggest buildings
full of
chinless wonders

who drown
in their own
useless evenings

they move
like cows
in big tuxedos

making deals,
shelley fabares
and
the neutron bomb

this is
government.

old drunks
with personalised
number plates
for falling
into
the right car.

NOTHING AT ALL

i've talked away
my best ideas.

i move through
some landscape
looking for places
i cannot locate.

what can
i tell you?
what can i say?

these little
erratic signals,
little poems,

they're
all there is.

i would like
to have
'staying power'
or become
'a model
of consistency'

but i like
words like
'useless'

nothing
occurs to me
at all.

ADELAIDE

antarctic winds.
winter
in adelaide.

i wait
for change.
unable
to bring it on.

sometimes
i feel sick
walking home.

life here
is regular,
i go
to work.

over here
in artland

they are writing
about 'art'
again

they call it
'art language'

and are
concerned
for those
who don't
speak it.

in the east
the ocean
affects
the way
we think
the way
we move
and talk

the tiny hills
that surround
this town
mark the spot
where
the future
stops.

with no future
there's no history.

but the hills
are colourful.

in this town
ideas
come second
to funding.

old broken academics
say they are
'stuck in adelaide'
and, at parties,
yearn for paris.

the poetry scene
is insular,
eats itself,
is well-heeled
and uses words
like 'burgeoning.'

i drink
a little
every day.

i walk
the dog.

old film makers
play croquet.
old actors
act.

a kind of
concussion,
a paralysis,
sets in

ken searle
paints
a budgerigar
on whistler's
mother's head.

ABOUT A DEATH

driving round
  in a car
    full of tears.

we are separate.
  we are not
    ourselves.
everything
  is useless,
      as never before,
        as if induced
            by drugs.

between seasons,
  tiny leaves
      falling
        in cold sunlight.

we have nothing to do.
  we drink and cry
  and the long day
  and the small habits
  accentuate the loss.

we sleep
  with phantoms.
we tread
  on our own shadows.

little memories
  are like
      nuclear waste.

EVERY AMERICAN WINS A PRIZE

executive cocktail lounge.
new earrings.
double martinis.
mary tyler-moore.

'i'm going
    into real estate.
there's a whole world
        out there
and
    i want to
        sell some of it.'

the dukes of hazzard
on the home stretch

the urge,
    in the rented customline,
        to drive into
            the oncoming headlights

regaining consciousness
    with the radio on
    'fame. i'm going to live forever.'
    under the crushed-up
                dashboard.

but
    the most sickening
            thing
is   don lane
    singing
        'Imagine.'

I REMEMBER DEXEDRINE. 1970

one of those days
i'm saying things
i don't usually say
and
verboballistic comets
are shooting
from my mouth
thinking rapidly
like films
run backwards
i race through the rain
like a rocket
to a dance hall
men and women there
are taking off
their shirts
and
they are friendly
but i wonder
what's inside them
ill in the head
by now
but not thinking
'this awful music'
'this stupid rain'
and then
there is something
the saxophone does
and i have to leave.
the taxi driver
looks right through me

and sees
the corroded rubber hose
that is
my bronchial tubes
i cough like a car
and
drop the money
all over the seat.
in the kitchen
i polish the brass taps
for a few hours.
on the table
a scrap of paper
where i have written
'the blank bullet
in the firing squad
is one image
i am sick of'
i tear it up
and later
i feel i KNOW
what REALLY happens
between
dark and daylight
but i've forgotten
by breakfast
which i can't eat.

DUMB PIANOS
POEMS 1982

.

'NOT EVEN OUR
SHADOWS COLLIDE'

all night and every night
  for six nights
no sleep and not unhappy
  (although i am
          i am unhappy)

as weight drops from me
trains rattle past
at dawn
the business week opens
there are things to do

i am thinking
and thinking of what
        she said

she said   she wanted
love without sex
  and i lied
i said   i can do that
and what i meant
was that terrible song
'I Can't Stop Loving You'
which
  is all i can say

anyway   i am the one
who stated it
who has done it to her
it's all too bad
        too bad

so i want to be someone else
a visual artist, a painter,
at least be able to draw
   more than anything
and to sleep
      one day
         to sleep

and not
   to wake
or maybe to fall
from a hill
   on a windy day
anything to end
      this waking
this big awake
   which
i could even call
      'wretched'
and know it's true

it would be some relief
   to cry
to cry again
   like last night
   full of sadness
      and nausea
and   quiet tears
   just rolling out
and down
   onto the pillow

in someone else's bed
in someone else's room

where i cry
  about someone else
  and they are all
  different people
and i'm crying for myself

and reading books
and staring all night
  and checking
  the crease
in the centre
  of my forehead
in the mirror
every few hours
and rubbing my hands
  across my face
around my eyes
  especially
and sighing
  with this new, this awful

and it started with noise
  ends with worry.

A DAY FOR SWING

saturday afternoon. dog barks in my suburb.
not much traffic.

i put on a record.   pete fountain
at the bateau lounge. late 1950s clarinet.
a kind of wonderful swing. the day is temperate.
it's a 'just-a-dance' day.

lately i've been saying what i think
about music.   i'm a fool
for a yodel and a good saxophone.

and anything alfresco pleases me.

and the person next door
has remembered the piano. she plays the classics.
this happens every now and then. sometimes though,
weeks pass by without a sound.

but today is made for swing.

RAIN STORY

when it's very still
  very quiet
    like this morning

i am in my bed
  with no cigarettes

the light
  enters sideways.
makes small shadows

nothing else
  is like
    this moment.

rain,   the rain
  i wanted,
is raining for me

almost perfect

and this
is for your birthday
  so
i remember you

seriously.

and the colour
  i think about now,
    about you,

is pale lemon

i don't know
  if you like it

pale lemon

hoping you do
  i open the window

    wide

and everything
  alters
because of that.

we talk a lot

    but
i wouldn't dare
  to say
    'cheer up'

ever
  again

once though
  i said

'your eyes are like my dog's'

i lose
fountain pens
  and gloves

never see them
   again

but
it doesn't
  really matter

anyway
  that's what i say

it doesn't matter.

always.

and clocks.
  dumb clocks.
    dumb exquisite clocks.

dumb violins.

dumb pianos

they
  make me
    feel like singing,

today anyway,
  in my bed.

a small morning.

ever stupid.
  ever happy.
and it's all terrific,
    really

especially
  driving
    through
a million near-misses

it's like that,
  isn't it.

really though,
  you deserve more
    than this,

on this occasion.
a tommy leonetti record.
  an answering service.
    a ticket south,
      west, north,
        east?

bed socks?

but this
  is the gift,

it is for you.
  it can't be helped.

it's coming
  from happiness,
    not from fun.

not even
  from
    show business.

simply

  happiness

    for you

that's
  the gift
    i guess,

but
  sometimes

your hand
  passes through
    your hair

and
  surely
    you wonder?

KEEP IT QUIET
PROSE 1983 - 1987

NOT LIKE THIS

It happened this morning. In the bank. I felt like a dog on heat. He had a torn t-shirt. He was slim, dark hair, not tall. He looked like he'd been on something last night. Pale and slightly sweaty. Are you listening? When I came home the planes were flying in the wrong direction. I said, the planes were flying in the wrong direction. Are you listening to me? I don't think you heard what I just said. Do I always have to repeat everything? Why don't you ever listen? I was talking about what happened this morning. I don't know what I'm going to do. I always feel like this in summer. These feelings. It's lust it's not desire it's desire turning to lust turning to anger. What will I do? You're not really listening to me. I can tell when you have something else on your mind and I go on talking. It happens a lot - I don't understand you. You're always so distracted you know - always looking away, always. This is important to me. Not that you'd care anyway. I should just talk to the dog. I'm trying to tell you about these feelings you know. I'm sure he'd been on something last night. I should have brought him home with me. This always happens to me in summer. I won't be able to stand it. Not like this.

NIGHTS LIKE DOTS

Saturday.
We sat in the hotel and his eyes shone like the glasses. Raining, and in a place we didn't want to be and I couldn't cross the street and leave him there, believing he would never phone. I knew I was never going to give up drinking even when I couldn't afford it. So we sat there. No money. And we ordered more Coruba rum and talked like travellers. No saxophones. Dreams were made of sweat and that was about all. Nothing romantic, none of that. Just thanks for the drinks and Saturday night was coming up like a storm over Darlinghurst.

Tuesday.
I'll tell you the worst things about myself and then you can tell me the worst things about yourself and that way we can decide to avoid any kind of conflict. Like this song - 'There's just a meanness in this world' followed by an extremely pathetic harmonica. And by pathetic I do mean pathos and this is certainly one of the very worst things about myself. I tend to go overboard for really pathetic music.

Monday.
This is the place from which we part. We live out the nights. Everything is clear. In focus, crisp, sharply lit. Here I listen to myself constantly. In this house the imagery is quiet. I never relax. I scrutinise myself. I examine photographs of friends. Everyone is hurt. In the photographs everyone is happy. One of us is lonely. We hold ourselves forward to the

camera. And tonight when she asked me to talk about it. The feeling that I can never express the way things feel. And I am breaking. I can do anything and nothing. Sad. Contemplative. Breaking, without tears. To slip into sleep. Slip away. Not connected, not interested. Tired of love, like Lou Reed.

Thursday.
The pale pink carnations. The pleasure. In the Tower I travel backwards above Sydney and feel displaced. Later, my lips swell up. You come on my lips, on my tongue. In 'The White Hotel' the woman offers her breasts to the dinner guests. At the table a man drinks from her breasts. This excites me. Rose petals fall from the sky onto the lake.

A THOUSAND TEARS

In Memory of Jane Jesse Rider Conachie
and Rienie Van Dinteren

'To try to write love is to confront the muck of language.'
                    - Roland Barthes: 'A Lovers Discourse'

'The moment I am born I am old enough to die.'

                    - James Hillman: 'Suicide & The Soul'

There is no need to worry. Love and death are the
only things worth living for. The mysterious reasons
we remain alive. The skeleton rises from the under-
world clutching a deep red rose. 'And the bone from
the depths of stone become bone.' This skeleton, this
female revenant, reminds us - 'enchantment leads to
doom.' We do not panic. We stand still, together,
looking at life and death. The soul is in the rose.
From the depths, death makes her entrance and the
rage to live subsides.

Grand, profound, beyond words, death dissolves the
daily into nonsense; all kinds of things; miracles and
mistakes. The soul is in the rose. And the spirit is a
leaf in the wind. The spirit is urgent and makes
mistakes. The spirit moves from the alone to the
alone. We meditate, we eat only vegetables, we seek
clairvoyance. From all alone in the dark to all alone
in the light.

We return. We go back. We tread on our own
shadows. Love is a phenomenon of the spirit and it
leads us back. The arrow falls where it will. We can
only follow. Pieces of paper in the wind.

We fall in love. We swoon. We fall into a faint. We faint away from the body. We fall into a physical hint of dying. Into a borderline condition. The heart still pumps the blood. Like being rendered unconscious by anaesthesia. Love takes us far away from ourselves and into ourselves. We faint in love. And, briefly, we dwell in the slim peripheries of consciousness.

We faint into and away from the empirical trash of the personal world.

James Hillman again: 'The first community are the dead, the ancestors, the community of souls. We don't die alone. Death is communal, entering the community of the dead, and these dead are always present in the heart. They are like presences. They may be the ground of love. An underworld ground. Maybe love comes to us from the dead.'

Falling and fainting into love, into a sudden glimpse of a fresh and dismal entropy. We forage through the heart's residual debris. Picking through the tip we find our bits of scrap and coloured stone. From these we piece together a mosaic - for the other, a picture of ourselves.

We scrape and fold and turn the muck of language into tentative whisperings of image. Life carries love through fantastic sceneries and vacant lots. Death is a moment.

Pier Paolo Pasolini: 'and a thousand tears gush
from every pore of my body,
from my eyes to my fingertips,
from the roots of my hair to
my chest,
a great weeping gushing out
even before being understood
almost before the grief itself.'

There is no need to worry.

THINGS

There's the telephone. There's the tape deck. There's the bookshelf, the piano, the kerosene heater. There's the empty room I enter like a shadow. There are the postcards from Venice, from Adelaide, Cooktown and Melbourne.

Here comes the music. Here comes the mood.

There's the scrabble set, the pack of cards, the game of solitaire I gave her for her birthday. It seemed appropriate to the independence she offered. There's the record collection, the tapes and address books. There's the tatty bunch of wattle I picked near Stanmore Station.

Here comes the way I felt about her. The way I feel now. Here comes confusion. Here comes sadness. Here comes anger. Here comes love. Here comes my best influence - the way she started to smoke cigarettes. She smoked them beautifully. Strikingly adept. Stunning and sophisticated, like the sixties.

There's the video deck. There are the piles of foolscap folders. There's the Bartok she taught me to play. There's the collection of pictures of cows.

There's the hallway. There's the small grey room with the grey door, closed.

Here comes the future. Here comes travel and all kinds of things.

YOU

Saturday afternoon. Late. Summer. Yoy don't know it. You're at the beach. You're reading a book. You're in the park. You're arranging a ticket to Europe. You're at the markets. You don't know it this Saturday afternoon. You're driving back from Bondi with your friends. You are not thinking about me. You are asleep in your room. You are dreaming. You are not drinking alcohol. You are laughing with your friends. You are reading Baudrillard and you are intoxicated with ideas. With speech. You are cutting up pieces of Super 8 film. You are in the dark. In the cinema. Desire drains you. You don't answer the telephone. You want to be alone. You are surrounded. This Saturday afternoon. You are making notes in the margins of photocopied articles. You are sitting in your garden looking at the tiny white roses and thinking of London, of Canada, of racing cars, of flying an aeroplane. You don't know it. You are feeling hot and you are loving Sydney in Summer. You are walking in the markets. You are buying new clothes and you look so different. You are not thinking. You are my projection. You are your own desire. You are feeling sick and you are fragile. You are withdrawing from your past addictions. You are leaving your brief addiction to my body behind you. You are reading a road map and explaining your particular sense of the map to a friend who is fascinated. You don't know it, late, this Saturday. You are away in the cool shade of your room. You are moving papers around on your desk and you don't know that I am looking at a photograph of you.

LITTLE EPISODES

She is a passenger in a car. She is silent. She can't be bothered. At the zebra crossing the driver makes an attempt at conversation, 'Look at that cardigan. What a wonderful blue.' She says nothing. Like an old existentialist, she can't be bothered.

She walks away into the sunset many years after a painting by Turner. Someone had suggested that we were here, in life, between something we could not remember or know and something ahead, also unknown. That suggestion had altered the way she lived.

Anne said. 'You know, of course, you can never really **attain** anything - everything just keeps changing.'

'You don't do very much. What exactly do you do?' She thought about the question on the Literature Board application form which asks how many hours a week are spent writing. Laurie said he always answers '24 hours a day.' And she remembered that sentence 'An artist's life always begins tomorrow' but she decided against cleverness and said, 'You're right - nothing much.'

One night she is walking alone. Little sonatas in her pulse. In the street every house is a tiny beacon, all possible and fantastic.

When they are drinking together they discuss great titles for poems or books. A painter recounts his months of solitude in a tent in the country, and she calls it 'Repressed In The Bush.' Chris tells her about a book he has read and says 'It's a terribly symbolic novel.' They decide that's a wonderful title -'A Terribly Symbolic Novel.' Someone else says, 'What about "Things We've Lost."' And he means political 'things', causes, ideals, but Morgan says, 'I lost a really good dress once.' They are very drunk and the poet says 'It's a headline universe.'

One of the writers says that she went to the bank to ask for a loan. The bank manager asked 'What are your assets?' Truthfully, she replied 'My talent and my prospects.' He leaned into the desk and said 'But my dear, **this** is a BANK.'

And one day in the middle of a large grey drift she received a letter from a friend who said he no longer wanted 'to work in the art field - it's just garbage' and that he wasn't doing anything at all about 'The Future.' She thought of her own future as a few more lines on her face, a few more bits of writing (if she was lucky or able) and more drinks. She was growing up slowly. She had not grown up old.

She watched some of the poets of her generation turn into journalists. She said to a friend 'I have seen the best minds of my generation become journalists' and they laughed. Some days later she heard her friend repeat this at a party.

I suppose it shouldn't be published. And I know it will be. The text book success stories, the homilies like 'Well, when you feel angry you should go for a walk.'

In the sleepless night she realizes that she is accountable to no one except herself. She stops answering the telephone. She wants to become a recluse.

And these are the little episodes she will write:

1: We travelled interstate together. On the plane she told me that her ex-husband had been impotent and that once she found receipts from a brothel in his wallet. And that, she said, was during the nineteen-seventies when everyone discussed their relationships and developed ideologies around sexual behaviour. She told me she had been shocked by this. She was that type of person and she liked to disclose intimate details about her lovers.

2: They walked through the city in the rain. They were looking for someone who had disappeared. She said 'I don't like trouble' and he responded 'Neither do I.' What she disliked was having to be so vigilant about other peoples' sensitivities.

It was a small incident. She lived without intent. She turned away from you to talk with someone else and you got up and left, you vanished. You vanished into your dislike for her and she searched for you and waited. And waited tearfully. Held to ransom by your powerful and desperate absence.

At one point, while she waited, she imagined your skinny white body stretched out on the floor of a hotel bathroom.

She suffers from a kind of tropism - her response to you is constant, always on. She is waiting and she takes your crumpled shirt from the back of the chair and hangs it on a coathanger. As a mother would. And that's one way she cares for you.

And when you return she will say 'I feel we belong together. I don't always understand you,' and you will reply 'You're a lost cause.'

THIS PLACE
POEMS 1987 - 1990

IN THE DARK

'in a country that doesn't laugh
but wipes things clean'

everyone becomes a stranger
looking after only themselves
everything worth saying
is silenced   and after that
you sit by yourself everywhere
and you miss the connection
for dinner   with the one
who talks endlessly about himself
like a novelist on a grant
all the abandoned children
are there in the dark and little
brown cockroaches are crawling
through their bookshelves
they have thrown away the baygon
because of ozone depletion
all the abandoned children
behaving like telephones
waiting in perpetual availability
'it's interesting,' they say,
'those coins cost more to make
than they are worth.'

LOCAL POEM

We make our way
  through this
    overbright city.

The mothers
  of the disappeared
    shadow our steps.

We look up
  at nothing
here
  in the shade
    in Bond's piazza.

Where do we get
  the passports
    now?

Too sober to cry,
  we don't notice
    the orchids
that are always
    there.

They're there
    for us
as we trample,
  drooling drooling,
    through the weeds.

In our suburbs
  the Pizza Huts
    are full.

THIS PLACE

we begin with this place
Double Island Point
as we must have
a beginning

we enter the wide landscape
we see a man in a hat
and an overcoat   running
making rude signs
sticking his thumb up

a raucous voice
rough as root vegetbles
sings a very sombre song

he runs   beside a swamp
and loses his hat
to the wind

this is the place
someone is slapping a face
bruising an arm   in
an agony
of misrepresentation

and here are the sleepers
who have spent hours
on details   who have
swept tiles   who have mopped
who have set radio alarm clocks

one mosquito slapped to death
Double Island Point
two empty beds

ROMAN RED

for Virginia Coventry

Only sometimes
  we move slowly
    in galleries,
clutching catalogues
and crawling along
  the art world
        walls
like people with
  terrible toothaches,

and then
  there's the movie
we see   when we look
  out at the airport
  away in the distance,
  the big red tail
    sticks up
between brown & grey shapes
  as the aeroplane
    taxis home.

The Italians
  would
  laugh like billy-o
to see us sip
  histamine-free wine
  and discuss
  wonderful colours
like   Roman red,

that could seem specious
  but, later,
  we are blessed
    by the nightmare kiss
        of whisky.

I struggle
  with the cigarettes
and you say
  'Hey   let's play
    that weirdo
      Stockhausen
          again,'

while we spend
  whole days
  painting the walls
    the wrong colour
in this
  small construction site
    of a poem.

THE LONG YEARS

'We act as if being alone were a problem
perhaps it is a fixed idea
like the fear of dying in summer
when you decompose more quickly.'
                    - Peter Handke

These are the long years and these years
are the years which pass quickly.
              These are the middle years.
These are the years when we realize
we have been going about living
              the hard way.

Remember driving at night
along Coronation Drive,
     beside the river.
Remember this as I remember it,

as I remember   the canvas fans
on the ceiling of the Renoir Cafe.
     I was sick with influenza,
you were going away to France
or, maybe, that time, you were going
elsewhere   and as I remember
the shade of the shabby fibro verandah
where you handed me your notes,
     written closely in pencil
on small pieces of paper, each page
a different size,   your notes
on existentialism   which I kept
in a small black folder in a cupboard
and which were lost,   later,
when I looked through the house

when I looked through the house
after everyone had died,
                    as I remember.

These are the long years
    when conversational moments stretch
into stories repeated and repeated
until everything, the whole lot, falls
into a kind of overwhelming sincerity
    and it is then   that I become
 so self-conscious   that I can
no longer hear what is being told to me.

Remember   the auditorium
in which no one believed,
 in which they performed,
 and the boy who had an erection
    halfway through his song,
        the clock on the classroom wall,
the mustard colour
  of a particular summer dress,
the patches of sweat behind the knees,
    the stifling afternoon heat,
the terrible poems which you took seriously,
and the way we caught ourselves
                    remembering.

Remember, if you wish,
that I meet with you, each time,
    these days   to honour
      the spirit of torn-up letters.

These have been long years -
    the unwritten letters would tell you this -

that, once, I was so very upset
　　that I hit myself on the head
　　　　with a shoe,
and that, just before then, before
becoming distressed,
　　I had been thinking about
　　the electronic staircase in Japan
　　where each step plays a musical note
　　when stepped upon,
and, earlier, that year,
I had placed a postcard on the windowsill
　　　above my table -
a detail from Lorenzetti's painting
　　　'Allegory of Good Government,'
which I had seen in Siena in an earlier year.
It is the part of the picture
　　where Peace, Strength and Prudence
　　　sit together on a patterned couch -
they look relaxed, as if bored by government,
　Peace is so laconic she looks as if
　　she will fall to sleep
　　　and drop the olive twig she idly twirls.

As I remember　　　something
viewed from the back seat of the taxi -
　　a woman stood　　facing
　　　a cyclone wire fence,
　　tears made damp spots
　　on the straps of her sun dress,
the man placed his hand
　　on her pale bony back,
it was so very sad　　as serious
　　as if they might kiss.

Remember the present   or yesterday
as I remember   the idea of our lives
  and our actual lives,
and your use of that term,   again
  and again, 're-invention'
as a cure for loneliness
like watching a woman
with a string of pearls   slowly
  testing each one
    in the wine.

Here we are waiting   for the natural end,
  for some future winter   as I remember it,
and in these long years
we may eventually locate   the places
  beyond memory   in imagined countries,
  where English is the last language.